Bush-Republicans: Lies and Dirty Tricks

by
Richard Wickliffe

authorHOUSE®

AuthorHouse™
1663 Liberty Drive, Suite 200
Bloomington, IN 47403
www.authorhouse.com
Phone: 1-800-839-8640

First published by AuthorHouse 10/30/2008

ISBN: 978-1-4389-2675-9 (sc)

Printed in the United States of America
Bloomington, Indiana

This book is printed on acid-free paper.

Preface

In the early sixties America was the most loved and cherished nation on earth. A dollar was worth it's weight in gold, and the constitution was held above reproach regardless of the hate and suffering of it's black citizens. Even people like George Wallace backed down. Things were not perfect, but respect for law and order held on until that rebellious generation called (baby boomers) hippies changed the way of life.

This is what this book is all about, a spoiled rich man's son who seems to have to rebel against everything in his path. His right-wing Republican party has just become a rubber stamp.

You will discover why the Republicans seem to win and why the Democrats have been losing from 2001 - 2006.

You will also discover how George W. Bush followed in the footsteps of Adolf Hitler.

Bush's Map of the Third Reich

In 1935–1945, Germany was a highly industrialized nation, much the same as the United States. Yet the German people fell under the spell of a madman—Adolf Hitler—and gave him total control over their lives and their country. They paid a terrible price for giving their love and trust to that man. George Bush, with his right-wing, Watergate Plumbers is forcing America in the same direction. Who knows how far George W. Bush will go?

After 9/11, Americans who disagreed with Bush were treated as unpatriotic; even some members of Congress were afraid to vote against Bush and express their opinions. The Bush regime was appointed by a group of right-wing judges, and it was held together by lies and deceit. Bush hasn't yet gained the power that Hitler held, but his henchmen are working night and day in hopes of achieving that power.

The parallels between the two regimes are clear. Martin Bormann and Vice President Cheney are the deputy and assistant to Hitler and Bush. Much like Deputy Fuhrer Martin Bormann, who carried out Hitler's dirty work, Vice President Cheney did so by laying the foundation for the war in Iraq. The main difference is that Hitler did not have TV cheerleaders to cover his dirty work; he told the truth.

Hitler threatened the world the way George Bush threatened the "axis of evil." Leaders around the world were at Hitler's door begging for peace. Chamberlain, the then prime minister of England, and the Russian prime minister, among others were complying with Hitler's will. George W. Bush followed the same course. He applied the same tactics against Iraq, North Korea, Libya, and others.

Bush has surrounded himself with some of the most heinous extreme leftovers from the old Nixon Watergate lawbreakers—the Plumbers. One of Bush's most active lieutenants is Karl Rove; he is comparable to Hitler's propaganda minister, Joseph Goebbels. Both of these men were and are still shrewish, but they are good strategists. Let's not forget Bush's war minister, Donald Rumsfeld, who has more influence with Bush than SS minister Heinrich had with Hitler. Paul Wolfowitz and Condoleezza Rice are two of Bush's leading war hawks.

Of those who call themselves Republicans and Democrats, no two people think the same. Comparing President Bush with Adolf Hitler may seem unfair to some, but as an American, you must choose between the welfare of your country and your loyalty to public officials. If your love is so strong for God and country, then why would you support lawbreakers?

After coming to power in 1939, Hitler executed seventy-four officials in order to shock the German people into total obedience. The people were quick to overlook his faults and stood behind him. The Bush regime is to blame for the 9/11 deaths because of its refusal to act on intelligent information. Some believe that everything from 9/11 to the WMD and the war in Iraq were fabricated to create a condition of war. The right-wing extremists, led by Karl Rove, know how Americans rally around wartime presidents and how war boosts a president's ratings.

Americans are not stupid, but many are not aware of what the government is doing. There is a constitutional crisis, purposely instigated by greedy and power-hungry Republicans. Right-wing extremists have done more damage than good; their behavior is irrational. They are very rude, inconsiderate, and unrefined. They have no compassion for poor people and will kill to uphold their extreme views. This is the same reason the Nazis killed—to protect their extreme way of life .Many right-wing Americans are willing to sacrifice their loved ones to keep George W. Bush in office. Some of the most arrogant are found in the U.S. Congress, and most of our federal courts have shown a bias toward right-wing Republicans.

Remember when the Republican Party was called the party of dirty tricks? That was when the news media and the Democrats were not intimidated by the arrogant Republicans. That was when liberals were proud of who they were and the Democrats welcomed them. Today the party of dirty tricks has infiltrated the liberals' party, trying to plant undercovers in the 2004 election to undermine the Democrats. The dirty tricks were intended to create an unelectable frontrunner who George W. Bush could beat. Dr. Dean was one of the leaders, an outsider, unknown to most people. Yet he was millions of dollars ahead of other well-known candidates. Was it possible that the right-wingers were planting money in Dr. Dean's fund? Anything is possible with Karl Rove.

Because we have to live under the Bush regime for another four years, the worst is yet to come. The Republican Party was once a respectable group of statesmen such as Senator Javes, Senator Dukeson, Mister Ford, and others—leaders. The GOP started downhill after the rescue mission in the desert failed, killing several men and causing President Carter to lose the election. Under the leadership of President Reagan, the United States was selling guns for hostages and committing other unlawful acts. At the same time, George H. W. Bush, the CIA chief, issued a denial, stating that he was not in Europe during the Iran-Contra affair and had nothing to do with freeing the hostages for Reagan.

No one ever wondered why George H.W. Bush chose of all people, Dan Quayle as his running mate? This man was George Bush's trump card; he knew that if Congress discovered his wrongdoings and impeached him, who would want Dan Quayle as president? A dirty trick, but Congress was forced to tolerate Bush for four years.

During the eight years of President Clinton, the schemers had time to plot their dirty tricks to take over the three branches of government and try to change the presidents' time limit. Who are these right-wing thugs? Why were they not discovered? They use loopholes to get around the law, but most of the time they just don't give a damn. Dirty strategists such as Karl Rove will circumvent laws, even if the rules and laws are their own. Most right-wing schemers are ex-military, some are from the CIA and FBI, and some are simply right-wing radicals.

Many people don't see activity at the Bush White House as a normal government function. With George Bush as president, the activity there is more like a cult, and Bush is the guru, pulling strings. Every Republican supporter is subject to the rules of the guru. The party worshipers are giving him praise every day and night. Talk-show hosts on right-wing stations, their talk jockeys, are like ministers of the right-wing movement, preaching its hatred of the Democrats, liberals, and anyone who doesn't agree with George W. Bush. His doctrine is to seize control and use that power to overturn some standing laws. He fired the senate leader from Mississippi and appointed the GOP House speaker. Bush tried to intimidate Democratic Senator Daschle about going to war. Daschle told Bush off but later gave in to the right-wing pressure.

After taking over the White House, every spare moment was used against the voters in a power grab to boost his ratings. As Joseph Goebbels trashed the Jewish people as an excuse to kill; Bush's propaganda minister, Karl Rove, followed the Nazi road map and trashed the Democrats and liberals. Hillary Clinton's name was at the top of the list. Every new member of the extreme right of the party was rewarded with wealth and special privileges for their loyalty. It was like making a deal with the devil. The punishments for breaking the Bush rules were harsh. Tom DeLay the GOP boss and leader broke several house rules, threatening and bribing GOP congressmen on the House floor.

The Republican Party is not for every person, unless they were born to fit in; they are who they are. They identify with southern racists, militants, and highly aggressive war mongers. Colin Powell did not fit in with Condoleezza Rice and the others. The Republican Party is a party of corruption and dishonesty. They have led Americans to believe that they are pure in heart Christians.

In November 1933, after taking power, Hitler withdrew from the League of Nations. He told the people to trust him and that Democracy was superfluous. In September 2002, George W. Bush threatened to pull out of NATO if they didn't follow him in his plans of war.

There is another Bush/Hitler parallel. In the summer of 1930, the number of unemployed in Germany was up to three million. Hitler wanted war to boost his ratings and help the economic recovery.

Everyone knows that George W. Bush robbed the U.S. treasury of billions of dollars through his tax cuts. Bush claimed there was too much surplus; he gave most to the rich and big business, but the poor got nothing. He created the largest deficit in history and said that a big deficit is good for the economy. In December 2002, over three million workers lost their jobs. To make it even worse, the Bush government refused to extend the unemployment payments. But the worst is yet to come; the extremists will leave some awful scars behind when they leave office. Their presence in the White House will not serve justice or show respect for other branches of government

I believe that George W. Bush's main reason for coming to Washington was to revenge his father, old man Bush, whom Saddam tried to kill.

Gorge W. Bush resented Bill Clinton's success after Clinton defeated his dad, and Bush started destroying every legacy of Clinton he could find. After giving away billions of surplus dollars from Clinton's administration—most was given to his cronies and his big-business friends—Bush had already made plans to boost his poll rating. But the suspicious terrorist strike on New York fulfilled his plans. His approval rating shot up. The terrorized Americans jumped on the Bush bandwagon for safety.

After the invasion of Afghanistan, Bush wanted a higher approval rating. He had Americans eating out of his hand like frightened children, so now he could do anything he wanted. War plans had been made to invade Iraq, but the UN needed information about the weapons of mass destruction (WMD) there. No one believed the war tales Bush had sold to Congress except for the few small countries who felt threatened. Adolf Hitler pulled the aame bluff on the Europeans in 1939.

Colin Powell was the only one in the Bush administration who could sell the WMD lies to the UN. Powell was an honorable man who gave it all as a payback to the Bush family.

The war in Iraq was not enough for Bush to remain high in the polls. For that reason, another war plan was made against two other Middle Eastern countries: Syria and Iran. Bush had Americans believing that Syria had Iraq's WMD and they were supplying the terrorist with weapons to kill Americans. Keep an eye on the Texas cowboy! Bush is going to challenge the Syrians for his next gunfight at the OK Corral, giving them forty-eight hours to get out of town!

The Democrats have become too liberal and tolerant. Too much of anything can be worse than too little. Without some guidelines and meaningful standards, the old cliché of doing your own thing has no merit; it is the same as living a life without morals. The right wing has branded Democrats as living on the edge of sin, saying that they support liberals and liberals encourage immorality. "Do your own thing" was the lifestyle of the 1960s hippies. Charles Manson led his old death squad, when men were sleeping with their children. Some became homosexual, transsexual, bisexual, or rapists, but all these people—even rapists—are human and deserve those rights. Right-wing Republicans have a real problem trying to stretch their imagination to understand that people should marry whomever they want. Where do we draw the line, should man marry his sister or marry a dog?

Right-wingers are not always wrong, but they never take time to do what's right. It's because of their natural tendencies that they behave the way they do. Republicans are so infantile in their behavior, they turn everything into some kind of childish game, such as color codes and terrorists—their newest term is combatants. I served two years in Germany and never heard those terms. All we knew was that they were the enemy; in real life there are no color codes. The Bush White House is a place of schemers and dirty tricks that keep Americans on edge and fearful.

"Only George W. Bush can protect you," if you let them tell it.

One of Bush's leading handymen was the then house majority leader, Tom DeLay, from Texas. This man's arrogant behavior is typical of a right-wing Republicans and their abuse of power. Tom DeLay is under a criminal investigation for improperly using corporate money to finance a takeover of both the Texas capitol and the U.S. House of Representatives *(L.A. Times)*. What makes Republicans so outrageous is their greed. They had full control of the White House, the House, the Senate, and even the Texas Senate; what more could they want? The Bush White House has done more damage to this country than any other group since the time of slavery! If the Republicans are allowed to go on unchecked for four more years, God help us all! Our only hope is in the Democrats, but their hands are tied and they have been shut out of the power play. They have been so timid lately, we wonder whether they will have the guts to stand and fight or run. The American people love their freedom, but if we keep these Republicans in office, we will lose everything, including checks and balances and above all, our freedom.

Republicans are very good at inciting incidents that appear to be natural; they will keep you in the dark, not knowing what to expect next. Right-wing Republicans' first priority is to appear to be good people: "We are on your side, but everything else is secondary, including freedom, love, health, and welfare." Republicans despise those terms with a passion.

No one hates the government more than right-wingers, yet they want control of government for themselves. In the 1990s, the right-wing Republicans displayed so much hatred toward the government that it drew their kind out of the woodwork. They incited an antigovernment movement among the radicals and rednecks; some formed their own armies called militias. Up in the hills of the Midwest, they fought pitched battles against authority. Some of their breakaway members turned terrorist and blew up a federal building killing 168 adults and children—the Oklahoma City bombing. These are not the kind of people you want for your protectors.

At one time Republicans stood for a party of principle, of doing the right thing. But those people of principle are not there anymore. The party is now in the hands of corrupt right-wing Republicans, the grassroots voters who vote for anyone who raises the most hell. It excites them. They are led to believe that the hard-nosed Republicans are fighting for the right thing. Not any more; the right wing wants total governmental control. George Bush has been struggling for three years to gain that power hold. As a matter of fact, it came to that when they passed the giveaway $86 billion package and the medical care bill. That was when the Democrats were shut out of the process. Tom DeLay was the majority leader, and he threatened a GOP congressman on the House floor. Is that the kind of government Americans want? You can see the similarities between the Bush and Hitler regimes. Most of the GOP is a parallel to the building of the 1930–1940 Nazi party.

Religious intoxication led to the fate of the followers of Jim Jones. The followers of George Bush seem to be just as drunk. They all seem politically intoxicated on right-wing garbage. Republicans are very good at covering their dirt. Rush Limbaugh, their chief mudslinger, preaches right-wing trash. Rush Limbaugh may sound like a saint; to the contrary, that man is a dopehead with a thousand-dollar-a-day dope habit.

When the twin towers were hit on 9/11, George Bush tried to intimidate the world with his cowboy threats, "You are either with us, or you are against us!" Knowing what America had gone through, everyone wanted to help. But Bush tried to use the tragedy as an excuse to start a war and bully the UN into helping his cause.

George W. Bush and his right-hand man, Karl Rove has been following Hitler's road map. "Mein Kampf," the same strategies that were used by Hitler's SS are now being use by Bush's troopers across the country. People were jailed without bail and their homes were wire tapped without a warrant. In September 1933, the Nazis had made a fine art of staging enormous spectacles to inspire cheering crowds with Hitler's SS Troopers. Power-hungry men love staging their popularity around men in uniform. Bush staged his popularity on the USS *Abraham* aircraft carrier, wearing a uniform. He cowardly visited a staged meeting of troops claiming to be in Iraq. The magician Karl Rove can make things happen.

The Europeans are not as naïve as most Americans when it comes to politics. Most Americans will buy anything that has the religious or political flavor of their taste. Jim Jones's followers gave up everything because he promised them a miracle, in the same way that the right-wing extremists believe George Bush can walk on water. The Europeans and Asians have learned not to trust every politician. In 2003 most Americans were leaning to the right. Most were not aware of the right-wing plot to take over and change the status quo.

War of Vengeance

The White House will be even harder to take back. The reason is, the Republicans are tough and tricky and will not comply with voting rules.

"The war of vengeance was George Bush's main priority; everything else had to wait," said O'Neil, to the subcommittee Chairman. He went on and said that Iraq and Saddam Hussein were his top orders. Bush believed that if his father had finished the war against Saddam, he would have completed his eight years. Bush believed that Iraq would be just a pushover. One year later, Bush's dream of a three-day war and four more years after his re-election was up for grabs.

Starting from January 14, 2004, everything the Republicans did would be strictly political. Winning the next election was more important than the lives of those five hundred or more young men and women. Most right-wing Republicans would be willing to give up even more lives, if it would keep them in office.

The Republican Party is a party of shrewd, simple people with childlike behavior. When Arnold Schwarzenegger, for example, won the election for governor of California, his childlike demeanor was disgusting. These simple people can be as malicious as they are simple. Their extreme behavior appeals to hateful people and racists like the Nazi party. They are also capable of many of the same crimes. During the Watergate scandal, Nixon's attorney general's wife was found dead because she talked too much.

Their plot was to overthrow the status quo, it was a right-wing takeover to abolish the Constitution. Bush made his first move in ways above suspicion when he asked for national security legislation. The new law gave Bush dictatorial power when Congress yielded checks and balances to the White House. The Bush people tried to downplay the new power grab, saying that it was necessary to fight terrorists. But the only terrorists since 9/11 have been right-wing homegrown extremists.

Lincoln's 1863 Gettysburg Address was the start of the Republican party's rise to power. Now, 143 years later, the good old party of Lincoln has seen its best days. "The government of the people, by the people, for the people, shall not perish from the earth." Now the GOP is going downhill, dragging the Constitution along with it. The Bush Republicans have shown no respect for the office of the president of the United States. Bill Clinton lied about sex, and the right-wingers impeached him. But Bush and Chaney both lied about 9/11 and about WMD; they claimed that Saddam was supplying Bin Laden with weapons. Clinton's lies hurt no one, but in 2003, Bush and Chaney's lies sent over several hundred young Americans to die—so that Bush's rating would go up! Will Bush and Chaney face impeachment for their lies?

The whole Republican party is a party of vice and corruption. How can they stand to look themselves in the mirror?

George W. Bush tried to switch our attention from senseless killing in Iraq to the color-coded terror scare. We have had only two al-Qaeda attacks, but we have had more from our own right-wing terrorists here at home. Several churches were blown up in the South; another bomb went off at the Olympics; two clinics were blown up; the federal building in Oklahoma was blown up, killing 168 people including babies and children; and the Unabomber killed several people. The right-wing Republicans are responsible for these criminals' acts. Some of their leading senators and congressmen were demonstrating their hatred of big government, abortions, doctors, clinics, big spenders, and unbalanced budgets. They preached their right-wing garbage and their extremists came out of the woodworks.

The Democrats are not in power at this time; the ruling GOP are the ones to watch. They have not allowed the congressional process to work, and the House and Senate leaders have shown their arrogance toward the Democrats and anyone who disagreed with Bush and the right-wing movement. Senator Byrd from West Virginia, one of the most respect historians and constitutional scholars in the Senate, was shut down from further interrogation to save face for the party by chairman Ted Stevens, one of the GOP's most arrogant Senate leaders! Take a long look and see their demeanor, their hard-nosed expression of domination.

This coming election, George W. Bush should get a taste of his own dirty tricks for stealing the 2000 election from the American people. It was a right-wing conspiracy, including the chief justice, who should have let the state courts handle the election problem.

This is a serious problem with the right-wing conservatives who have not shown any respect for human rights and the laws of this country. Anything goes in order to gain power. If the courts break the law, then the Democrats should not obey an unjust law! Vice President Gore gave in too quickly and didn't have the guts to stand and protect his turf. That is another problem with the Democrats; they should learn to fight fire with fire! They seem to be so intimidated by the right-wing bullies that they lose their will to fight.

The Bush regime's foreign policies are failing and will soon be bogged down in a political backlash. If the Democrats had stood their ground, Bush would not have rushed into war, and the war in Afghanistan would have been over, and bin Laden would be hanging from a rope.

The Democrats controlled the Senate at that time and should not have given in to Bush's pre-emptive war. Tom Daschle and House Minority Leader Gephardt went against their party and gave Bush their votes. He had a strong hold on the right-wing GOP and the many voters who later gave Bush what he wanted—in both houses of Congress. After their sweeping election, Bush became even more like Hitler; he started making threats of war on other countries while tightening the noose on his political enemies!

George W. Bush may look dumb, but his administration was protected by his propaganda squad and a group called the Plumbers. The Plumbers have no limits and will go to any extreme to have their way. During an election year, there are usually fatal accidents that happen only to Democrats. Some Democrats have resigned their offices rather than work under arrogant Republican leadership. Their leadership is characterized by those in the White House; just as with Hitler when he controlled Nazi Germany, flexing their muscles is a show of power.

The Republicans and their sympathizers are characterized by strict regimentation. They all seem to think, talk, and even act the same. There is not much difference between them and the old racist southerners, which is another reason Republicans are accused of racism and the reason most southern politicians prefer the Republican party.

The true, lawful, patriotic American must remain focused, or this country will not survive intact. Not if this abusive leader has his way. According to the *Washington Post*, a right-wing Republican, Grover Norquist, is making plans to keep Republicans in power. He has been traveling across the country in a right-wing conspiracy with other radical to oppose federal laws! And George W. Bush has already started his movement to drive more nails into the coffins of the Democrats.

David Kay, the WMD inspector, said there were no weapons and there never were. Bush chose this man, but for political reasons, he refused to accept his findings.

Later the Republicans held a committee hearing as a cover for George Bush and his illegal pre-emptive war. The right-wing committee members were not interested in the truth. They tried to threaten O'Neil into telling them what they wanted him to say. President Bush may not be too smart, but to his Republican cronies, it does not matter.

Yet to come is a feeling about this coming election 2006. The Democrats have been too complacent about the Republicans. For that reason, another dirty trick can be expected as they try overturn the outcome of this election. Right-wing Republicans are by nature a vengeful people with many dirty tricks up their sleeves They are also an irrational group who will support any self-destructive ideology if it's right-wing conservative. This is what makes them so dangerous! Notice how the Democratic leaders are playing up to the hostile Republicans.

Just keep your eyes open for some kind of arrogant right-wing movement. If they try again, this time blood may be spilled. The Democrats have had it with their dirty tricks. The election of 2000 was a deliberate act of conceit and arrogance by the right-wing extremist Republicans and the chief justice. This kind of judge is not worthy of such honor, and history will be their witness.

President-elect Al Gore may have gotten what he deserved (the high court). He didn't have the will to fight for his rights. The Democrats need a strong leader with guts, like Harry Truman, Jack Kennedy, and Bill Clinton, who was a good president even though he showed weakness in his appeasing remarks about the WMD. The Republicans are very much aware how humble the Democrats have become. If they had been more of an assertive party, the court would have remained neutral and Al Gore would have won.

Exploiting 9/11

Al Gore was not the only victim of right-wing trickery. The tragedy of 9/11 tops them all; it was a godsend for the Bush people and living hell for the Democrats while they struggled to find answers. After 9/11, the Republicans acted as if they were having a picnic. George W. Bush exploited the tragedy for every political advantage he could find, and the horrors of 9/11 were played down for Bush to capture center stage. It was a sickening sight to watch how Bush wrapped himself in the flag as the people cheer, not as much for the brave firemen as for Bush.

The Bush regime is controlled by high-pressure groups with ready cash, airline tickets, and other goods from the lobbyists and even from Mexico and Israel. A spokesman from Spain told a reporter on C-SPAN that Bush's war was not fought on behalf of the United States, but for the state of Israel. He went on to say, "Why does everyone seem to talk around

Israel as if it does not exist?" (March 21, 2004)The man was right; ever since the Six-Day War, when Israel blatantly attacked a U.S. ship and killed several servicemen, that demonstrated the carte blanche for Israel to do as they damn please! Only the right-wing Republicans would permit killing of their own people to please another right-wing government. That kind of sacrifice happened in Iraq; one hundred fifty thousand young lives are in the line of fire, but why, for what, and for whom?

Colin Powell's mission was to go to the Middle East to help keep the peace after learning that Israel was terrorizing the Palestinian people. They were killing people and ripping down homes and buildings with tanks and helicopters. Instead of rushing to help save lives, Colin Powell stopped and spent a few days in Spain. Bush came on TV while the bloodbath was flashing across the airwaves and acted as if he was pleased with the peace trip. Sixty percent of the Israeli people did not believe that the hawkish Sharon and his right-wing army was planning for a peace settlement because of the United States' involvement.

This Republican White House is the most corrupt office since Richard Nixon. Adolf Hitler was a madman and a killer, but he had more common sense than Bush, with all of his talk shows, flunkies, and cheerleaders. Yet Bush has a mysteriously strong hold over his cronies and party leaders.

For the last twenty-five years, the GOP was the party of no taxes, expenditures, and balanced budgets. But all that has changed to a party of greed— obnoxious and peremptory. They have given away billions and billions of dollars to big oil companies, friends, and the corrupt puppets of the Iraq war.

The Bush-Cheney, regime does not tolerate insubordination. Unruly party members, those who crossed the line, were punished. And no one really knows the truth behind their power.

Deranged

President Bush is up to his neck in one of the most heinous criminal acts since the Civil War. Only a president could have pulled it off without being questioned.

The man is seriously ill, and no one seems to notice his unreasonable behaviors. He has psychotic tendencies but has sublimated them brilliantly. The duty of the president is to serve and protect, so his oath of office placed him above suspicion. Bush arrogantly exposed his sick motives, but no one believed what they saw or what he was doing. He is a man of vengeance and retribution, and as strange as it seems, his main victims are the government and the American people.

He has his own sick reasons for defiling and dishonoring the office of president and worst of all, the people who served under his command. Bush hadn't forgotten what the voters did to his right-wing Republicans in the 2006 election. He retaliated against the government when he threw open American doors and its solvency to big business and his crony nations around the world. Bush sold out his border agents to favor Mexicans and drug dealers when he jailed his agents and rewarded the drug dealers. He also defiled the Constitution when he ordered wire tapping and outsourcing our jobs.

Republicans have been very successful in their takeover of the White House and Congress, but not because of their honesty. Republican has become the party of deception, trickery, and double-dealing. They have led most Americans to believe they are god-sent. They also tricked the voters, saying that it is unpatriotic to speak out against the government at a time of war! The Bush government's double-dealing is their main source of success. Robbing the U.S. treasury of the over $400 billion surplus. At that time most Americans were on his bandwagon.

Most Americans took Bush at his word, believing that everyone would get their share of the tax money. But only the rich received kickbacks, and the poor got only double-talk. He paid off big business, the rich, and his cronies. Bush said only the rich pay most of the taxes, but the poor pay the same taxes as the rich at the gas stations, for licenses, for clothing, and for other costs of living.

At that time the Bush people and the right-wing Congress fell completely under the White House's control. Bush rewarded them all after looting social security and Medicare. And let's not forget, he promised no child would be left behind. Even at this time, he is still fighting against funds for schools, against his own words of promise.

Republicans has always despised the federal government because of its power and strict laws. Whenever they gain power, they use it against whatever rules and regulations they feel are a threat to their control. Their right-wing TV and radio cronies, such as FOX, will justify whatever they do, even murder. Some of the most arrogant of them all are members of Congress. The Senate has it share, but not like the House leaders, such as Tom DeLay. At times the Republicans try to show some dignity, such as when they threw a special Congressional ceremony honoring the ninety-second birthday of a special black lady, Ms. Dorothy Height, with a congressional gold medal of honor . They led the ceremony because the GOP was in power and they were trying to be politically correct.

Republicans come across like people from another planet to most Democrats, probably because of their dogface expression. They show no respect for

Democrats because liberal behavior is too selfish and lacks logic and common sense. For that one reason, Republicans have been winning most elections.

Bush appointed a commission, which was supposed to be bipartisan, to investigate the 9/11 hijackings. In other words, it was supposed to find the truth, even if it was against their party; let the chips fall where they may. But that was not the case when it came to Richard Clarke, the former top counterterrorism agent.

Mr. Clarke told the commission that the White House refused to take the war on terrorism seriously. The president was more focused on Iraq, and 9/11 was pushed aside. The Republicans lost their cool and started to criticize Clarke. This is the way they are; the oversight committee was too rigid for the Republican chairman and his partisanship came out full blast. From that day on, the Clarke family became a punching bag for the right-wing cronies.

There was an article in the *Washington Post National* about *Rise of the Vulcans: The History of Bush's War Cabinet,* by James Mann. The backgrounds of these six people explain their foreign policy. These Vulcans are: Donald Rumsfeld, Dick Cheney, Colin Powell, Richard Armitage, Condoleezza Rice, and Paul Wolfowitz. Much of their behavior is also an extension of Old Man Bush's thinking. "The new world order" would carry out this plan with or without the other nations. In their sick minds, they feel that power gives them the right to change the world. They feel that the ends justify the means, regardless of who is hurt in the process. Their dogmatic arrogance is what makes them so dangerous. More than three thousand people in New York and more than two thousand young military men and women sacrificed their lives for George W. Bush. They are not only cold-hearted but also unreasonable.

They have poor judgment when making important decisions. What sensible people would attempt to impeach a sitting president for having sex? They should have known they didn't have the votes. This kind of behavior is childish and shows no foresight. What could you expect from Republicans?

The Bush and his cronies came to Washington for one reason: to change the world to his liking, in other words, for the same reason Hitler came to Berlin. Bush has been watching John Wayne too long; his theatrical behavior was used on Saddam Hussein. He even pulled a high noon to meet him at the OK Corral. You have forty-eight hours to get out of town! That was Bush's way of declaring a Bush war.

There are so many loose ends in this Bush administration with his right-wing congressional puppets, including his African American helpers. Are they for real or a joke? Could there be any merits; if so, what are they? Black Republicans are just as misguided as the white Republicans, and more important, they are not recognized on the same level. Congressman Watts, from Oklahoma, resigned for that reason. Black Republicans are used as tools rather than as party members. Bush named Colin Powell as secretary of state before he was elected to get black votes. Bush made other plans after he was elected, and these plans were his most cold-blooded of all.

The Bush government was built on and by schemers. They wanted more than just being a president; they wanted the dressing also, such as the popularity to serve eight years—not four like Bush's father. They knew that wartime presidents are the most popular and powerful of all president. Richard Clarke told the committee that when he first briefed Condoleezza Rice about al-Qaeda at a January 2001 meeting, she acted as if she didn't know who he was. But she knew all about al-Qaeda; she just didn't want to spoil their plans to look the other way and let al-Qaeda do their thing, not knowing it would be as destructive as 9/11 was. That strike on New York was an answer to Bush's prayers.

The Bush people probably had no idea that al-Qaeda was coming after them and would be so destructive. They may have been willing to take a soft strike, but 9/11 was too close to home; it almost got the White House. But that didn't stop the Bush war hawks, who saw the damage as collateral.

Bush has been accused of so many unlawful acts, and if they are later found to be true, who will he answer to? George W. Bush, at this time, stands above the law. A Republican Congress will not impeach a Republican president! Will the Democrats do anything if they win the next 2006 election? No, they are too wimpy and timid.

Bush couldn't have asked for any more than what he has dictated from his right-wing Congress. In 2004, the panic-stricken Americans were still grieving after 9/11 and gave Bush everything he asked for. He was their Big Brother and their savior. To make it even worse, the Democratic Congress was also standing in line after losing the 2004 election. Most Americans were not aware that the killing in Iraq was orchestrated by the right-wing Republicans. Their schemers are very shrewd, with many dirty tricks on their playing field. Competing against the

Republicans is like trying to outfox Satan, who plots while you are asleep.

Why have the Republicans been so effective in convincing the voters to vote for them, and why have the Democrats been on the losing end? For the same reason Al Gore lost to Bush. Gore didn't fight back; he let them have their way. Although Al Gore couldn't have stopped them if he had wanted to, the Democrats would have been more successful.

Times have changed; the political battlefield is where you must fight fire with fire. The Democrats have been trying too hard to be politically correct. Senators like Joe Biden, Kennedy, and Speaker Pelosi are typical appeasers. Kissing the ass of a rude president is senseless and a waste of time. Republicans knows the Democrats' behavior—they are too shy and timid to stand their ground and fight back. The leading Democrats don't seem aware of their self-destructive behavior; they even allow the Republicans to dictate their political strategy and give them permission to stigmatize their party's politics.

You'll hear the right-wingers say, "Dr. Dean is too liberal," or "She is too pushy or moderate" for their party. Democrats are too busy defending themselves against insults and name calling from the rude GOP party. This is another way they disrespect Democrats.

Remember when Bill Clinton was accused of a sex scandal? At that time Clinton was alone; his party and his many friends had turned against him. Joe Lieberman and several other Democratic senators turned on him. Clinton was dead wrong for doing it in the White House, although he committed no crime. That was a sign of weakness, and it opened the doors for impeachment. The Republicans would never have turned against one of their people.

George W. Bush is caught in a web of scandals and lies, and some could be treason. Every Republican in Washington is fighting to uphold his name. The Democrats could learn something from this display of loyalty. Republicans will not speak against each other; they fight as a unit. They treat Democrats the way the Democrats treat themselves. The Democrats should start referring to Republicans in the same manner as the Republicans refer to them. Give them a taste of their own name-calling medicine. The Republicans are party freaks, every one. If they want to stay in the party, they must put party before self and country, "Together we stand, divided we fall." Most Democrats get wrapped up in political correctness, but playing the game of trying to look honest at the expense of the party is the reason Democrats are losing.

Bush is gambling on an old Republican trick of trying to refine the roughneck cowboy kind of politics. Karl Rove knows that Ronald Reagan was that type; it worked for him and it seems to be working for George W. Bush. The roughneck bullying kind of politics has attracted the redneck type—low educated, rural people. In the same way, it attracts the big-city right-wing extremist—You know the kind, the war gamers, gung-ho, like the SWAT teams, state troopers, and Navy seals, anything that has to do with war, law enforcement, or power.

At one time, the Democratic party was the poor person's dream, but today it's a life-and-death struggle for Democrats to hold on to the little power they have. The Democrats have a weakness for backpedaling and brownnosing the hateful right-wing Republicans. Some have been straddling the fence, such as Senator Miller, Senator Lieberman, Senator Biden, and Junior Senator Feinstein, from California. They are too conservative and are not dependable as leading members of the Democratic party. They can't be trusted; they are the weakest link in the chain of party leaders.

Democrats have another weakness: they give away their campaign strategies. The right wing will use those tactics against the candidates. It's okay to talk about your plans but not the execution of the plans. Republicans will try and use whatever you say against you. Not only what was said, but also anything Democrats do will be forever trashed by the right-wingers, and it's worth it to them; many times it works. They are masters in the skill of mudslinging.

The Republicans, despite of their boasts about the war, are suffocating in a no-win war. People can be very dangerous in such a situation, grabbing hold of anything to survive a loss.

Democrats must learn to be assertive when confronted or challenged by the conniving Republicans. Most Republicans are loudmouths but cowards when confronted or put to the test by facts and truth. They will fold like the Nazis did when their racial supremacy was challenged.

Bush's behavior many times has surpassed the Nazi arrogance of Hitler and has become the worst of all the forty-three presidents. He was the only president to blatantly overstep his constitutional oath of office.

His first two years were the most critical and frightening in his campaign for more power. Like Adolf Hitler, everything he did was highly glorified to maintain his grip on the people. Bush also learned a special art from the Nazis, the art of deception.

Without those skills, he would have had to act within the law.

The Bush people are goose-stepping in Hitler's tracks.

Bush is above mistakes, waging wars is like playing video games to him, causing human suffering and pain without apology. Yet he claims a relationship with God and that God wants him to control the world. Besides his Godly and Nazi connections, Bush has another calculating scheme in progress. Between May 2003 and May 2004, the Bush attack machine maneuvered a deceptive scheme of reverse psychology with the use of kiss-and tell book scandals. They are plotting a reverse reaction in the polls. Notice that all of the so-called kiss-and-tell scandal books were endorsed by George Bush before printing.

Now all of the president's men and women are part of the scheme in their denial of the truth. The Bush schemes are still working and seem to be on the rise. Regardless of his wrongdoings, Bush acts as if nothing had happened. He depends on his right-wing talk radio and FOX network cheerleaders.

Bush was just a figurehead for the right-wing hardliners; now the Republicans party worships his image although he screwed up at times, like the time he pulled most of the troops out of Afghanistan to fight his war in Iraq. This time he got his priorities mixed up and went after the wrong people. Now al-Qaeda and bin Laden are plotting to kill more Americans. Bush was too quick to forget the more than three thousand Americans killed in the Twin Towers in New York. His twisted mind led him to believe that Saddam was behind the Twin Towers tragedy. The real killers are now laughing at the Bush's WMD blunders. Only a fool would shoot his foot to stop a pain.

Sixty percent of the American people can't comprehend the Bush juggernaut. His behavior is something that no one would expect to come from a U.S. president. For that reason, he gets by with more than his share. What did he do with the billion-dollar surplus from the Clinton administration? And why did Bush, after depleting the surplus treasury and cutting the lines of revenue to the government, then start a war that required billions of dollars?

A right-wing talk-show host was blabbing about the unruly Islamic extremists and said, "They should show some appreciation of our boys dying to make them free." Right-wing people cannot come up with the proper answer; they are too self-righteous and hypocritical. Let them try this on for size, to see how it fits: If a powerful Islamic nation were to overwhelm the United States' military forces to free Americans from a government the Islamic people felt was evil and corrupt and exchange it for their kind of government and religious practices, how would Republicans react? They wouldn't have to answer that question; their reaction is obvious!

First of all, Iraq didn't ask for American intrusion; they were happy as they were. How would the radical right-wing feel if invading forces captured George W. Bush and treated him the way the U.S. Army did Saddam? Now you people, stop passing the blame on to God! Does God condone killing? Now all the blood of those thousands of Iraqi people is on the hands of Bush and his cronies. They must also, above all, bear the blame for the thousands of young men and women in the U.S. military who died to keep Bush in office.

There was no practical or legitimate reason for the attack on the people of Iraq. Bush had hatred for only Saddam, not for the people of Iraq. Someone will have to pay for those senseless crimes against humanity sooner than you think. Bush's cheerleaders may cover for most of his unthinkable activities, but fate cannot be fooled.

Bush and his Republican flunkies took part in a gas-oil conspiracy with Saudi Arabia, defrauding the oil market of billions of dollars to get elected in November 2004. This is what you call a dirty trick. Every dirty trick, lies, fraud, conspiracy, even manslaughter, is a crime against humanity if done for political reasons. Saddam was not a threat to anyone outside of Iraq. Bush and his flunkies made up that story about WMD as an excuse to attack Iraq and rob them of their oil, but it all backfired on them. All of those people died in vain; what kind of a man would exchange body bags for political votes? You can't get any lower than a snake!

This is the man claiming to do God's works. Right-wing Republicans are not as honest as they try to pretend they are. It had been over a year when Bush declared the Iraq War was over. Now the Republican leaders are stuck with Bush's overstated declaration of ceasefire.

Bush's War

George W. Bush calls himself a Christian and an evangelical warlord against those he declares to be the axis of evil. The truth is, Bush is more of a con man and street hustler. If not, he would not have been able to con his commanding officer when he went AWOL for six months. He used the Bible as a cover for all the rotten acts he committed against others.

If Bush would give as much time to important government projects as he has given to running games, America wouldn't be in Iraq today. Every move he makes is a calculating scheme to cover shady activities such as the WMD lies and pretending that Condoleezza Rice was his personal security adviser. If that were true, why did she slip and referred to Bush as her husband? She is constantly defending his mistakes and blunders as the war goes from bad to worse.

Chairman Henry Hyde doesn't like sexual misconduct in the White House. Will there be another impeachment hearing?

The Democrats must be ready to stand toe to toe in their fight for both houses of Congress and the White-House. They will try to lead you to make self-destructive mistakes; in the 2004 election, Senator John Kerry was led into that trap by Cheney, who kept him on the defense for several days. Senator Kerry should have made a short statement and let it go. His military record didn't need defending; it could have stood on its own merits. It was a calculated trick to keep Senator Kerry on the defense and keep him from attacking Bush's war record. At that time, everything was going wrong on the battlefield, and U.S. forces were caught brutalizing and torturing prisoners of war. It is a fact that the behavior of the troops reflects the sentiment and attitudes of their leaders. This is the first time that kind of treatment was used against prisoners of war. This proves that George W. Bush has serious psychological problems that have affected his judgment.

No reasonable president would send his troops into battle without a planned strategy. And what practical leader would keep his troops on an ill-fated course without any adjustment of plans and strategy? Bush takes pride in staying the course. That is Bush's way of showing power and leadership. Karl Rove keeps reminding Bush how to behave in order to mislead the people, although he seems to be running out of ideas for making lies into truths and truths into lies. Staying the course is not strength but weakness.

Time is running out on the GOP leaders, including their right-wing Congress who was part of the rightwing cover-up. Both Senate and House leaders refused to investigate and helped cover possible crime and wrong doings. In March 2006, Bush's polls were down to 34 percent and the death toll was up to twenty-three hundred young lives and counting.

Their party is in a political quagmire, trying to find their way out of their own blunders. Bush has several strikes against him, WMD, sea ports, the war, and Katrina; Rove is under investigation, and Chaney almost killed a man. And on top of that, his token black advisor was caught stealing. It's not easy to find black Republicans without some character flaws. Black or white, why would a person choose a group that is out of touch with reality? Republicans are people with self-destructive values who find more joy on the edge starvation and poverty in the hopes of proving that extreme right-wingism is worth the sacrifice. But only the poor trailer trash and rednecks are the real die-harders.

The so-called hardliners of the Republican party and the good old boys like Chaney, Senator Hatch, Strom Thurmond, and others like them set the right-wing rules but never told their followers that lying, cheating, and stealing from the poor and taxpayers is worse than going hungry.

Have you ever heard a Republican official complain about cutting the wages of low-income workers? The GOP voters send their people to Washington on their behalf, believing that their work is against evil and they are doing the right thing. Seeing that the Exxon Oil, General Electric, Bank of America, Boren Aircraft, Fox TV, and the like are getting the best breaks, I don't believe the right-wing poor people really understand the true purpose of their congressmen in Washington. If they only knew, these representatives were not there on behalf of the common and poor people, but instead were there for the rich, the wealthy, and above all, big business.

Every time Republicans are elected, the working class and blue-collar employees suffer at the hands of lobbyists, big business, and dishonest politicians, such people as Vice President Chaney, who made a deal with a California utility cartel in a price-fixing plot. Vice President Spiro Agnew was forced to resign for his crooked dealings. Ronald Reagan was caught red-handed selling guns to the enemy for profit to support some South American terrorist group.

On March 19, 2006, the Republicans found themselves bogged down in lawsuits and other unlawful dealings. Caught off guard, the bullies were running like pack-rats. There were no coattails to hang on to. Bush is now a lame duck who should be running himself and should be impeached for his wrongdoings.

The Democrats should have stepped up their strategy and taken advantage of the right-wing political mayhem. But the Democrats were still playing the political correctness game, and on top of that, their leaders didn't have the guts to even try.

At one time George W. Bush had the people eating out of his hands, and when he pushed the color-code button or shout terror, the people would shake like frightened rabbits. Maybe sooner or later, the Americans will wake up to his right-wing terror tricks and the Democrats will be in power.

Democratic Unity

Republicans' acts of boldness is what gives them an edge. Even when the liberals are right, their kind of politics drives the Democrats into a nerve-wracking silence. They seem to fear fighting back and giving the Republicans a taste of their own rudeness. There have been some heated floor fights in the House and Senate. The right-wingers can get downright nasty when there is any talk or movement that will impose any rules that could affect the business industry.

Al Gore refused to permit several House Democrat to protest the election of George W. Bush. The vote counting was held in the House of Representatives; Al Gore was the president of the Senate and showed the world how politically correct he was by stepping on the rights of his own people and defending the man who stole the election from him.

His reason was that no members of the Senate had the guts to permit a representative to speak on their behalf. If it was the other way around, a Republican

Senate president would have refused to take part in the vote counting, and the whole House would had been all over the place.

Who else would do something like that but a good old Washington-brownnosing Democrat? Who is on trial every day trying to please the other side of the House and Senate? When they took back the House, the speaker and the Senate president couldn't wait to get over to Bush's office—why?

It was easy for Al Gore to stand up against his own party members, but he didn't have the guts to stand and fight for himself. There are reasons to fear the radical right-wing; they'll go to almost any extreme to get even and demonize their political opponents. Could that be part of the reason the Democrats lose so often?

Republicans learn to work as a unit, even if they hate each other's guts; however, things are not as smooth as they seem. They are held together by force and back-slapping, payoffs, hush money, bribes, and even threats.

Bush had to come clean and tell the truth about the WMD and that 9/11 had no connection to Iraq. But even to this day, many diehard Bush cronies are still trying to fabricate them together. He should have been censured; instead, the Democrats let them cover up his stupid mistake.

Colin Powell was force to lie to the United Nations to justify a pre-emptive war against Iraq, although Powell was misled by his boss and friends, including Condoleezza Rice. And the Democrats in the Senate and House lined up with the Republicans, except for a few Democrats, who voted no!

The Democrats should know that whatever plans they come up with, the Republicans' dirty-trick machine will try to sabotage it. When the Democrats come up with a good plan, don't worry about right-wing trashing. Just stand firm on your insight and your solutions and don't give them the power to drive .you into flip-flopping. That is their game, and don't forget their magic word, backfire. Don't say it if you don't mean it, but once you've said something, stand firm! Most of the time, it's best to ignore what they say you said or they will show a flip-flop. This is the way they think, and their childish behavior seems to work for them. Only schoolyard bullies stoop to this level of vengeance.

In his 2004 race for president, Senator Kerry made a mistake; he allowed them to force him into flip-flopping by taking controlling of his agenda. Senator Kerry's record was among the highest and needed no further explanation. In the political world, try to never get trapped into defending against a false accusation. Your political adversary's tactic is to gain points at your expense. Take control of your subject, not allowing the GOP to lead. The dominant factor of winning is intimidation; it can psych you out to the point of self-defeat. Intimidation causes anxiety which causes a negative response.

Intimidation is one of the main factors in winning in sports. Very seldom you'll see momentum on both sides; generally, when one side is up, the other goes down. When team A is scoring in front, and suddenly team B starts making a few three-pointers, then team A is psyched out by the sudden move. Then in the next quarter, the same can happen to them.

Democrats must keep their eyes open; not all arrogant people are Republicans. Democrats have their own kind, who bash each other to appease their GOP so-called friends. Republicans are the way they behave, the way they treat people, the way they appeal, and above all, the warmth of their heart is in the expression on their face.

Could that be the reason the Democrats fear the good old boys on the floor of Congress? The Democrats were forced to tolerate the Republicans. I believe the right-wingers probably had the same difficulties in trying to figure out why and how Democrats fight so often but soon kiss and make up.

Democrats see themselves as siblings and rivals not hate mongers, digging up dirt and Swift Boating other people.

Criminal Illegal Immigrants

I've just had my eightieth birthday, and I have seen it all. I've seen many presidents in my time, but I have never seen anyone like George W. Bush. He seems to have some kind of special control over the news media, TV, and radio. What will happen to Karl Rove? The prosecutor probably wont get to first base if Bush has his way. Right-wingers have always been deceitful bigots.

The Republicans probably didn't deserve it, but today they seem to welcome Senator Bilbo and other southern senators who brought racism to the GOP party. Therefore the southern racists felt more at home with the Republicans than with the Democrats. At that time, the Democrats were not afraid of losing, because of the strong leadership of those like LBJ, Sam Rayburn, and Hubert Humphrey. Democrats had better leadership at the time of the civil rights bill. The party was loaded down with southern racists, but got the bill passed, out of sixty-seven Democrats, forty-six voted yes; in the GOP, twenty-seven out of thirty-two voted yes for the 1964 civil rights bill.

The Republicans went from bad to worse when the old southern racists joined them because of the voting rights bill. The GOP had only thirty-three seats, and Democrats had sixty-seven. The old die-hard southerners did what they thought would stop black advancement. They wanted to see black Americans back in the cotton fields. The old southern bigots lost the fight, but deep down in what they call a heart, they haven't given up hope.

The American people were duped again and tricked into electing the same corrupt government again. This time they control everything, the White House, the courts, the House of Representatives, and the Senate, and corruption has intensified. The Democrats have been stripped of power, the right-wingers are having a field day, and the federal prosecuting attorney was dragging his feet.

America's election process is among the best, but it also has flaws. The system allows illegal immigrants to blackmail the Congress to get what they want. The 2006 election was a hot potato for Republicans. They have always voted their conscience regardless of political pressure. It took lots of guts to try to impeach a sitting president who had not committed any crime.

Will the Republicans give in to the bold illegal immigrants' threats, knowing that illegal immigrants can't vote? For the last five years, the GOP Congress voted for everything Bush asked for, until Bush stepped out of line and started to support the lawbreakers. Illegal trespassing is a serious offense. But the Democrats are more afraid of the illegal immigrants than the arrogant Republicans. Democrats will give them everything they ask for, even knowing that they can't vote.

That is the difference between Republicans and Democrats. Republicans are too dogmatic and macho to give in to threats and protests. The GOP and patriotism go hand in hand, if you let them tell it. The GOP sees America as a nation of laws and wants stronger laws to protect U.S. sovereignty. Democrats are also true Americans, but they have their own way of doing what has to be done. Democrats fight with feeling and emotion, except when politics are involved. This time they are with George W. Bush, who is trying to recruit more illegal immigrants. Bush talks about protecting Americans from the outside, but illegal immigrants can be terrorists too.

The Mexican president, Fox, and other Mexicans in California are making demands that illegal immigrants should be treated as citizens! "They just want to work." Sure, American citizens want jobs too. Now when illegals come in and work for less pay, they take jobs from Americans who deserve the first chance. Republicans are not buying that kind of talk. They want all illegal immigrants to go back and come through the front door like everyone else and not come over the back fence! Most black Democrats seem to lean with Bush and are not thinking about the consequences. Black children are being gunned down by illegal immigrants. Blacks and Democrats seem not to care; the only thing they care about is the 2006 votes.

The jails are full of ten Mexicans to every African American. They are killing anyone who stands in their way, even police. Many victims are their own people, especially their women, because the Mexican government prevents them from being arrested. If they came through the front door, criminals would be screened and sent back.

Most of the illegal immigrants in prison were criminals when they came, with the guts to march on Washington to try to bully the Congress, waving their flags.

The Republicans haven't given in to their threats, but black Democrats seem to sympathize with other minority causes. The Republicans sympathize only with their party! They don't have bleeding hearts for social causes. Illegal immigrants have shown their shrewdness and their kind of respect for America by the kind of flags they fly. Most were Mexican flags, and in East LA, some illegal immigrants pulled down the American flag and replaced it with a Mexican flag.

What are the two tough GOP members Representative John Kyl, from Arizona, and Senator Jeff Sessions planning on doing? They were leaders in the Republicans' fight against amnesty for illegal immigrants. Were they just blowing off steam, or was it just another right-wing bluff?

Whatever law they pass, there could be some bloodshed. Many of those illegal immigrants are criminals; many are from Columbia, Venezuela, and Mexico. How will Congress deal with all of these illegal immigrants? Make them all felons or find some other way out?

There are many questions that need answers. Illegal immigrants are just the tip of a menace problem. Bush, with all of the urgent things that need attending to, went all the way to the Arab nations, disturbing a hornet's nest. The people in such nations live with violence, and nothing pleases them more than vengeance and killing Americans. Over twenty-three hundred servicemen and servicewomen have been sacrificed, just so Bush could settle his score with Saddam.

Staying the Course

The Congress has been in the hands of right-wing Republicans for going on seven years. They are much aware of Bush's leadership and the blunders he is still making, but Congress refuses to question his behavior. After five bloody years of street fighting in Iraq, the only plan Bush has is just staying the course.

There is talk of Bush's obsession with the corporate world taking control of some of his oversized government. Bush's erratic behavior could lead to his father's new world order ideas about one world government. These right-wingers care more for big business than for the victims of 9/11, the military, the troops in Iraq, and the fifty thousand homeless in New Orleans.

This is the man America voted for, even after four years of corruption, blunders, and lies. America is in serious trouble in the hands of a man who wants to outsource American industry. The right-wingers want to dismantle it piece by piece.

The American people should never again elect another spoiled brat, a son of a rich family. Most children of rich people grow up with the mentality of a spoiled brat. They are used to getting their way and have a know-it-all, stubborn attitude. The two spoiled sons of Saddam Hussein were allowed to have their way, beating and touching to satisfy their egos. The two Bush brothers fit the same shoes.

Bush had been on a warpath when he declared war on the axis of evil. He then called Taylor, the warlord of Liberia, and told him to pack up and get out of Liberia. Taylor didn't think twice; he left, saving the country from death and destruction.

Bush tries to do the right thing, but he gets his priorities mixed up and comes out on the wrong side. His advisors are even worse for not telling him the truth. They believe spending more revenue than what is coming in is the best way to balance the budget. This is why we are in debt to China, in the amount of hundreds of billions.

Since I started this book five years ago, there have been some changes in the Republican party. Some are leaning to the left; some have gone more to the extreme right. Some seem lost for position, but the rank-and-file Republicans are still holding the line. That could change too; it depends on the Mexican lobbyists. They are hard to predict when their jobs are on the line. The right-wing extremists see party loyalty as more important than jobs. The radical right-wingers are devoted Republicans—as if it were some kind of religious cult. Their social patriotism is mostly superficial and theoretical.

Now that the Democrats have taken over both houses of Congress, the hard-liners, the flag-waving, FOX TV and talk radio cheerleaders are at a loss.

Not all right-wing Republicans carry a bulldog's smiles and growl. Some of the normal-looking right-wingers are the most knavish. Someone like Sean Hannity comes across as a cocky, overbearing, conman. His Sunday show is set up as a verbal, high-tech lynching of black America, after destroying their lives and their political reputations, as with anyone else who disagrees with his extreme politics. Hannity, one of FOX's altar boys has a natural instinct to kill off the right-wing's enemies.

Their right-hand defender, Condoleezza Rice, still believes she is recognized among the right-wingers as one of them. Only George W. Bush recognizes Condoleezza Rice and Colin Powell as bona-fide black Republicans in good standing. That's because Bush is not a real right-winger himself. He is a maverick, and not as conservative as one may think. Call Rice what you want, she is stigmatized as a warmonger. How could an educated black woman with her kind of background sacrifice her reputation by taking part in a conspiracy to cover up WMD lies and supporting a first-strike war to kill women and children? Well, what can be expected from a black woman who sold out her race?

Bush's arrogant stance of staying the course has not changed any more than his decision to drop the hunt for bin Laden to go after Saddam Hussein. The secret behind that change is still a mystery. Let's go back to 9/11. Remember when all the planes were grounded, even the president's father was grounded, but there was a fleet of special planes that were permitted? Now guess who they were? It was the prince of Saudi Arabia, a close friend of the Bush family.

Why were they given special privileges? They feared retaliation because fifteen of the sixteen hijackers were Saudi Arabian citizens. Bin Laden's father is a member of the king of Saudi Arabia's family. Now do you see why Bush permitted the son of bin Laden To escape from Afghanistan into Pakistan? As a favor to the king's family. Bush felt they were the only victims of 9/11. How many U.S. soldiers have been sacrificed fighting a false war? You, the readers, must judge for yourself and ask why the family of the killers, the hijackers, were given special privileges.

New Era

In January of 2008, the Democrats were back in power of Congress, both houses, including two strong Democratic frontrunners. They are Senator Obama and Senator Hillary Clinton; both are running for the office of president. Politics is a dirty field to try one's luck. It became even dirtier when met with racism, when right-wing racists joined forces with racist Democrats to help destroy Senator Barack Obama, who happens to be African American.

I believe Senator Obama may have made a mistake by giving an interview to all stations, including FOX TV. They are the butchers of the right-wing party. They hate Democrats, and if the candidate is black, God have mercy! Senator Clinton's desperation for the top office has pushed her over into the right-wing camp; because of the Republicans' fear of Obama, they would prefer running against Hillary Clinton, whom they feel is less electable.

On Monday April 28, 2008, a dogmatic black preacher, Reverend Wright, has dominated the top news, not so much to try and clear up what he said, but to punish Obama for disagreeing with his choice of words.

Many African American ministers are not humble spiritual leaders. Their arrogance conflicts with their egos, and God is hung out to dry! "Thou shall not bear false witness against another human being." I hope Reverend Wright will realize the harm he has instigated, not only against Senator Obama, but also the American people, including African Americans and himself?

Few people understand what drives a preacher to overreact when preaching the gospel. It is the same as the Rolling Stones, James Brown, Little Richard, and the like. It is not what they call holy spirit. The true works of the holy spirit took place the day of Pentecost: Acts 1–3, when everyone started to shout, speaking in tongues; the holy spirit had come upon the people.

Republicans don't care about divine causes or about morality and righteousness any more than Reverend Wright does. You'd be surprised that the Grand Old Party of JFK has its own style of racism. There is difference between being racist and racism.

Racists are those who are out to do bodily harm, such as the KKK, the skinheads, and the Nazis. Racism is a slanderous act against a people who look and act different. Hillary Clinton, under desperate trials, has played the race card with a sense of guilt.

CNN has also stooped to the level of FOX in a blatant act of racism. The two stations knew the damage they were causing to Senator Obama's chances of winning against Senator Clinton. It was obvious what they were doing and why. They ran Reverend Wright's speeches sometimes five to six times an hour, over and over, Saturday, Sunday, Monday, and so on, through the first of May. This is a new era of progressive liberation but it is hard to overcome the taboo days of the pre-civil rights era, the days when it was a crime to place an image of a white woman and a black male in same frame or see such a thing without raising an eyebrow. Almost forty years have passed and that same old negative attitude toward a black male in connection with a white female seems to be intact and holding.

Remember when O. J. Simpson was found not guilty for the deaths of his ex-wife and friend? There was more uproar over that verdict than that of a white man who killed over twenty young black and white women, the Son of Sam killer. There have been several other white male murderers of the same kind, but after the trial, the media found something else to talk about.

The hostility toward African American males who are involved with white females hasn't changed at all. Remember the Lakers superstar Kobe Bryant's run-in with a young white hotel clerk, who claimed Kobe raped her? And Wesley Snipes, the only black star that plays romantic roles with many white women, was sentenced three times as many years at his trial than white men for the same offense. Bryant has been picked on by NBA officials time after time. Barack Obama has been tormented day after day by acts of racism, hate groups, and a preacher turned Uncle Tom.

Most people believe those groups are all involved in a conspiracy with Reverend Wright and right-wingers to help Hillary Clinton in her hopes of destroying Barack Obama's race for president. White men resent black men outdoing a white woman.

Human Rights and Dirty Tricks

May first is another day of Mexican illegal immigrants protesting for special privileges. No other group of people or ethnic group has ever asked for much, not even American citizens. These illegal immigrants are not citizens of this country and have no right to make demands without the power of conquest. They are behaving like illiterates, without any knowledge of civil rights laws and the constitutional structure; it's like a party crasher demanding more food. How will the Republicans respond to such boldness? No group can compare their suffering with the civil rights movement of African Americans. Black Americans are natural-born citizens and were denied equal rights with other Americans.

Such rights as women's rights, gays' rights, immigrants' rights, and others are not the same trials and tribulation of black Americans. Even to this day, many blacks are still on probation because of their skin color. For others whose skin color is light, their skin color acts as a shield. African Americans have nothing in common with others who brought their problems on themselves. Illegal immigrants have self-inflicted problems, yet they are asking for special enactments to legalize their self-made problems.

Will the Republican Party comply with standing laws, and what will the Democrats do? Democrats have control of Congress but haven't found the guts to do what has to be done.

American's most dangerous enemies are not the sleeper cells right now; keep an eye on the trustees of America's lifestyle of leisure. You know who they are? That May Day protest in 2007 was a wake-up call, a show of strength; "When we don't like your laws, we'll shut you down!" America has become too dependent on cheap labor. Republicans wanted cheap labor or slaves at the expense of immigration laws.

The 2008 May Day march in LA was nothing like 2007. They knew that their bluff didn't work; it only made things worse. The immigration officials have been cracking down all across the country on management and illegal immigrants.

The Mexican president, Fox, is so gobble in his unrefined manners that Bush was knocked off guard.

Both presidents pose serious problems for America, although President Fox is not aware that he is too dumb to realize that he is stupid. George W. Bush appears dumb, but his arrogance overshadows the little common sense he has. Now he is sharing his policy making on Mexican illegal immigrants with President Fox.

George W. Bush is out of touch with reality; at times he believes he is above the law and the Constitution is not valid without his consent. For the last five years, the Bush administration has been duping the American people and has destroyed our relationships with most world leaders, including many third-world countries. His erratic behavior has divided our political parties, class against class. He even tried to destroy the Democratic Party, but only Democratic Senator Daschle lost his seat.

Through some strange twist of fate, Bush found himself in the driver's seat of the world's most powerful country. He hasn't yet been able to comprehend the reality of his duties. All he seems to understand is his war and staying the course.

His unrestrained behavior and attitude has caused a rebellion among his cronies. He has abused his Republican Congress for over five years, and he demanded they cover for his blunders and misdeeds.

The 2006 Democratic Congress hasn't been much different. The White House raided a congressman's office knowing it was a conflict for power. The House leader at that time was a Republican who became upset and threatened an investigation.

Up to May 30, 2006, the Republican House held their first oversight hearing, after five long years, claiming it was an abuse of power. One representative spoke of impeachment, but when the Democrats took over the House of Representatives, Speaker Pelosi let it be known that their heads were down low with their tails between their legs, that impeachment was off the table, leaving the crooked politicians at their own mercy.

Democrats were disappointed with the Democratic leaders for giving in to the right–wingers. On February 9, 2004, *Newsweek* ran a story with the headline: "Will Anyone Pay the Political Fallout?" Cheney, Rumsfeld, Rice, and the others were all involved in the WMD intelligence scandal. Senator Reed and Speaker Pelosi both went against their promise to clean house. The right-wing lawbreakers are just as safe as they were when Republicans were in charge.

The DNC is having a hard time trying to raise more money now. When Republicans controlled the Congress, they claimed to be strict Christians, but they show more love for the unborn than they do for the living. From the time Bush took office, his first task was to latch on to his two Congressional leaders as part of his plans for total control.

Bush's world-domination ambitions were the same as those of Hitler and Karl Marx. His struggle for dictatorial power turned out to create a right-wing tyrant with only a 30 percent approval rating. His tyrannical behavior built up a strong backlash within his party:

UN Undersecretary Brown complained that Bush's hatchet man, Mr. Bolton, is trying to upset the business of the UN. Bush hasn't forgotten the UN's stand against his global threat of the axis of evil. The Secretary General was not moved by Bush's threats of "You're with us or against us." Right-wing Americans are almost as hateful as those throat-slashing Moslems

Democracy has never really worked the way it was design by the founders. America tolerated slavery for almost three hundred years and wanted three hundred more if possible. This kind of attitude is still in the minds of many white Americans.

Sean Hannity has an obsession with African Americans and their fight for dignity and fairness. His smears and slanderous remarks about Barack Obama and Reverend Wright prove what he has in store for Obama and other black Americans. The FOX political trapping machine has destroyed many of good faith.

Barack Obama is in deep trouble for trusting two other black people that I know of; Larry Elder is their number-one Tom, who came on bashing black Americans. The latter one tried to come on easy with his jive talk, claiming to be a civil rights lawyer. His name is not important as what he is trying to pull. This man built his show around the WMD; the feeling was mutual, trying like most Democrats being politically correct.

Knowing the mentality of right-wing people, he gave them what they love most—contempt for liberals, even though they were his own people. I listened to his show for a few months and cut him off when he tried to out-Tom Larry Elder, of all people.

The old talk radio serves two purposes, to sell products and to sharpen the hatred and racism. Joe Pine, the father of talk shows had the skill to rip anyone from limb to limb with his fast talk.

The Republican Party came up through the ranks of racism and hatred. Today it's high-tech and uses another tactic, the charm trap. Senator Obama was caught in those kiss-and-tell traps. Reverend Wright was the bait. They tried to finish him off. I hope Senator Obama will learn from that experience. As I said before, don't trust these Republicans; Hillary Clinton's desperation has caused her to trust the devil. She has started to flirt with hard-nosed right-wing Republicans Rush Limbaugh, O' Reilly, and the FOX news team. She thinks they are helping her because of Senator Obama, who is black. She is willing to play the race card, even with help from the devil.

More Lies and Dirty Tricks

Republicans are masters at lying and staging make-believe events, like when they exposed one of their CIA agents and passed the blame on to someone else. Bush's second election was fixed by his old right-wing Plumbers, who knew that the Democrats are too timid to investigate or stand and fight. Democrats have a hang-up about image. That was when Al Gore chose image over the office of president. Gore even stood against his own party members, blocking them from protesting the 2000 election of George W. Bush.

Democrats have been branded and stigmatized as immoral liberals because they support same-sex marriages, abortion, and so on. They have also been labeled as butt kissers, starting after LBJ left office. President Carter tried to play both sides of the fence; Bill Clinton went even further when he chose a Republican, Defense Minister Cohn, over hundreds of highly qualified Democrats. He then went out of his way to find two old grandmothers, one an unknown, unfamiliar woman, as secretary of state and attorney general. But they were too conservative and were a drag on the party.

Democratic leaders are too aloof, trying to prove themselves to be fair and honest. It is a stupid way to prove fairness. When Clinton was caught in a sex trap, not a single Democrat stood with him. Most Democrats backed away from him. Al Gore distanced himself from Clinton, even during his campaign.

These so-called politically correct games have cost the Democrats many seats. Ask Al Gore and Senator Daschel. Do the white men glorify their women when black men are involved? It's just an old southern feeling of keeping the black men in their place. Governor Faubus, of Arkansas, didn't let them forget. Some forty years later, some of that old racism still lingers.

Most Republicans, thrive on dirt; you name it, it's their game, from racism down to criminal acts. Representative Tom DeLay, Attorney General Gonzales, and several of his staff members were all caught in some kind of criminal act.

Most of these acts are committed by political appointees, and the party depends on who is in control and who the lawbreakers are. Democrats could not get to first base if they broke the law. Democrats are harder on their own than on Republicans, but they seem to fear the hard-nosed right-wingers and let them off the hook.

"Impeachment is off the table," said the new House leader. She made it known to everyone that the Democrats are not a vengeful party. The reason for that is an attempt to be politically correct. Keeping checks and balances, oversight, should keep the government honest, but that is not the case. The Democrats have gotten to be too sensitive about doing to them what they did to us. Why not? That is the duty of the ruling House and Senate, to investigate corruption and wrongdoing within the government.

At this time there have been crimes and misdemeanors; some could lead to high crimes. Much of the fault lies with two high-ranking chairmen of the judicial committee and the ways and means committee, the two most powerful committees in the House of Representatives. Representative John Conyers and Representative Charles Rangel, one of whom helped impeach Richard Nixon, have the ball in their hands, and you'd hardly know they are there. They are probably sitting with their feet on their desks enjoying their power, but they don't have guts to use it.

Senator McCain has been getting a free ride and free press, but his age won't let him get a free pass. He is now seventy-two, and when you reach that age, nature has beaten the hell out of you! Backaches, cramps, and loss of appetite; at that age, the aging process gets worse not better. Electing McCain as president would be re-electing George W. Bush. Four more years of George W. Bush could blow your mind!

Time is running out, and there is a deadline that must be solved for the Democrats: November 4, 2008. Barack Obama has the lead, but Hillary Clinton refuses to recognize the math and keeps going straight ahead without any chance of winning. The experts claim that Hillary Clinton is not trying to win at this stage. They said she has become a vicious enemy of the party, which she blames for losing to Obama. Her aim is to help Senator McCain smear Obama so McCain can win. Anyone except for Obama!

Not Hillary; could she really do something like that? There are all kind of rumors about her now; I believe she is trying recover from eight years of planning her dream. All of her hopes and dreams were destroyed by a newcomer, an unknown.

Govern by Law

Despite the Democrats' weaknesses, without their concern for social and other liberal programs, the United States would perish. Nothing concerns the Republicans more than keeping the big businesses fat, rich, and beyond government control. This is what happens to third-world countries like Mexico. Any government that is ruled by some business cartel is a victim of corruption.

This is what makes United States so great. The founding fathers were a step above average. They knew that any government without checks and balances would face many problems. Democracy is one of the best forms of government, but even with checks and balances, there are still challenges.

The Civil War, slavery, the overstepping of bounds by the judicial branch refusing to carry out its duties as lawmakers and legislating the law instead of interpreting the law. Checks and balances are ego blockers.

When Republicans are in power, checks and balances and the law are under constant attack. When Democrats are in office, they prosecute all lawbreakers, except high-ranking Republicans. How can they, when impeachment is off the table?

When Congress brought up the 2007 immigration bill, Senator Reed fought against every immigration bill that came up; it was not good enough for illegal immigrants. They spent too much time defending illegal aliens when there were more urgent problems to solve. New civil rights laws should be made to protect African Americans from police brutality. Blacks are not beaten, they are mauled before being shot to death. The city of Inglewood, California, one of the smaller cities in LA county, has one of the worst mauling and shooting records. There must be a law to protect African Americans fro hate thugs with badges to shoot and kill! There should be a misdemeanor against any public official who engages in unprovoked harassment and inflicting physical harm. There must be a felony law to prevent any public official from engaging or conspiring in the mauling and shooting of an unarmed African American. There should be capitol punishment for any law enforcer who engages or conspires in the shooting or beating to death of an unarmed African American!

Congress has the power to enact laws to protect citizens from harsh treatment by governmental agencies. Black citizens suffered three hundred years of the above treatment during slavery. Today's right-wing people pretend that it never happened or that even if it did, African Americans should be thankful that they are better off than those still living in Africa.

Not all right-wingers are Republicans. Hillary Clinton dug up the hard-nosed Democrats in blue-collar clothing. Most of them came here from the east and the Mediterranean, people whose lives revolve around the past or status quo. Change is not as important as their jobs, the area in which they live, and the people who look like them. In other words, the above is only part of the reason they all voted for Clinton over Obama; the reason is racism! If it was the other way around, they would all shout "playing the race card!" Some whites are competing with the scrub woman who sometimes takes a roll of toilet paper while the CEOs are stealing hundreds of millions dollars from their jobs. If caught, the poor scrubber will lose her job, but the CEO is seldom prosecuted.

George W. Bush is having an image problem; there aren't many places he can go to find a welcome, except for a few right-wing countries. John McCain, the Bush man who wants Bush's job but refuses to campaign with him, flew all the way to Israel just to smear the Democrats and Senator Obama. McCain came to Bush's defense or tried to exploit it for what it's worth.

In seven and a half years under Republican control, America has suffered a forty-year setback in civil rights and respect even among its next-door neighbors. The only people Bush feels comfortable around are his cronies and his army. There were two articles in the *Globe* about Bush's wife planning to divorce him because of his drinking and his relationship with Condoleezza Rice. The story ran twice, but no one picked it up out of fear of the right-wing revenge machine—the same group who attacked CBS's newsman who tried to expose Bush's military record, which noted the time when Bush went AWOL for six months.

This organized group operated in the same fashion as the SS Troopers. Not one media outlet came to the aid of their victims!

Senator Obama's dream of a perfect America could be as such, but the United States presidential elections are under attack. Special-interest groups are trying to influence the outcome of the primary race.

Hillary's white blue-collars didn't help that much, and Reverend Wright's display of arrogance seems to have helped Obama. The only things left are dirty tricks to manipulate the votes and poll numbers. But it is a federal offense to tamper with an election. I've noticed, as of May 18, 2008, Obama's poll numbers were down to third place, but a few weeks before, he was in first place, Clinton was in second, and McCain was in third place.

By changing Obama's poll count down below Senator McCain's numbers and putting Hillary's on top, they hope to influence the delegates in Hillary's favor.

If Hillary Clinton is involved in this kind of conspiracy, she doesn't deserve the office of U.S. senator! Congress has its share of liars and cheats, and they are trying to get rid of the one they have in the office of the president, Bush.

Some would say that Clinton would never do such thing. You cannot say she wants; she has tried everything else, why not this? Senator Clinton enjoys her white advantage over Obama, who may lose because he is not white enough. People in that part of the world are not intelligent enough to vote on issues; the only thing they understand is skin color.

I'm sure Hillary is using light face powder to make sure her skin appears whiter. She can't afford to lose those good old blue-collar boys, probably riding around in their pickup trucks, drinking beer!